Oprah Winfrey

TV Talk Show Host

by Margaret Beaton

 CHILDRENS PRESS®
CHICAGO

PICTURE ACKNOWLEDGMENTS

AP/Wide World Photos—pages 4, 10, 26, 65 (bottom), 66 (2 photos), 68 (2 photos), 69 (2 photos), 70 (2 photos), 71 (2 photos), 72, 84, 101

Nashville Banner Photo—page 14

Photos supplied by Steve Lowry—page 63 (top and bottom left)

Photos supplied by Donn Jones—pages 63 (bottom right), 64 (top left)

Courtesy Tennessee State University—pages 64 (top right and bottom), 67 (top left)

Courtesy WLS-TV—Page 65 (top)

UPI/Bettmann Newsphotos—pages 67 (top right and bottom)

Cover illustration by Len W. Meents

Library of Congress Cataloging-in-Publication Data

Beaton, Margaret.
  Oprah Winfrey, TV talk show host / by Margaret
Beaton.
    p.   cm. — (People of distinction)
  Includes index.
  Summary: Traces the life of the actress and talk show
host, from her childhood on a farm in Mississippi to her
achievements in broadcasting and film.
  ISBN 0-516-03270-4
  1. Winfrey, Oprah—Juvenile literature. 2. Television
personalities—United States—Biography—Juvenile
literature. 3. Motion picture actors and actresses—United
States—Biography—Juvenile literature. [1. Winfrey,
Oprah. 2. Television personalities. 3. Actors and actresses.
4. Afro-Americans—Biography.] I. Title. II. Series.
PN1992.4.W56B43   1990
791.45'092—dc20
[B]
[92]   90-2150
                                                           CIP
                                                            AC

Table of Contents

Chapter 1

SOMEONE WHO MAKES THINGS HAPPEN

An estimated sixteen million people watch Oprah's nationally broadcast talk show each day. One day she may interview runaway teens who are living on the streets, the next day battered wives or quarreling families. And then the following day she might have a fashion show.

Most of the Oprah Winfrey talk shows deal with serious subjects. Oprah feels that by having people talk about their problems on television, the audience—in the studio and at home—can understand their problems, too. There is always an expert of some sort (a psychologist, lawyer, or researcher) to give professional advice. The show receives many letters from viewers who have been helped through these programs.

Oprah's show has been enormously successful.

How did Oprah Winfrey get to the top of the ladder professionally and socially from her beginnings so far down the ladder—a barefoot farm girl from Mississippi, one of the poorest of the poor? Oprah is talented, but so are many poor children. She is nice looking, but many others were better looking.

Like most people who have become famous, Oprah Winfrey's success is due to a combination of talent, hard work, and determination. Starting off as an unwanted child born out of wedlock and living through years of child abuse, the odds of her being successful were very slim.

One turning point in her life came when Oprah was a teenager living in Nashville. Her father told her one day that there were three kinds of people in the world: those who made things happen; those who watched things happen; and those who didn't know what was happening. At that point, Oprah decided she was not going to be either of the last two kinds of people.

Certainly, Oprah Winfrey has been the kind of person who makes things happen. Her energy and drive have been remarkable. But even her extraordinary determination needed the right opportunities for expression.

Like all successful people—whether success is measured in material terms or just in terms of personal happiness— Oprah has been prepared to take advantage of opportunities

when they eventually came along. And she has worked hard
to make the most of them.

Vernon Winfrey owned a barbershop in Nashville, Tennessee.

Chapter 2

BEGINNING IN MISSISSIPPI

Oprah Winfrey's first audience was not unusual for a small child, particularly a lonely child. Like most children (lonely or not) she talked to her doll. But because she lived on a farm, her audience was extended to include cows, pigs, and chickens. And, like many children, she named all of them, and had animated conversations with them.

But by the time she was three years old, Oprah also could read to her little audience from one of the books her grandmother gave her. Often, her readings turned into performances as she recited Bible stories. Sometimes she mimicked her minister and delivered little sermons. When she was older and went to school, Oprah would continue to deliver impromptu "sermons" to the other students. This was a practice that didn't make her popular with the other children, and earned her the nickname of "The Preacher."

The other children weren't very fond of Oprah. They didn't like her church talk, and they resented her ability to read and write better than anyone else. They were very cruel and some would even spit at her. Oprah remembers as a child in Mississippi she was lonely, friendless, and unhappy. She had no brothers or sisters and her mother and father had left. She lived in the country with her grandmother on a farm. So the rejection of her new schoolmates hurt all the more.

Like many people in Mississippi, Oprah's grandmother was extremely poor. Mississippi was and still is one of the poorest states in the nation. In the 1950s, most of the black people in Mississippi lived as sharecroppers in conditions that had changed little since the time of slavery.

Oprah Winfrey was born on January 29, 1954, in Kosciusko, a small town in the center of Mississippi, seventy miles north of Jackson, the state capital. She was originally named Orpah, a name suggested by an aunt, after a character in the Bible. Orpah was Ruth's sister-in-law and is mentioned briefly in the Book of Ruth. But there was a mix-up in the letters, and Orpah became Oprah.

The farm Oprah lived on was off a dirt road on the outskirts of Kosciusko. Her grandmother owned the farm, which was very old and run-down. In the early 1950s when she lived there, there was still no indoor plumbing. An outhouse stood in back of the house, and a well was fifty yards away from the house. All the water they needed for drinking, cooking, and cleaning had to be drawn from this well. It was little Oprah's chore to bring in the water, every day, summer and winter. She also took the cows to pasture every morning and fed the hogs.

Most of the food Oprah and her grandmother ate was produced on the farm. Oprah never knew exactly how her grandmother got money. Extra money could have come from selling eggs from the chickens they kept, or from the sale of the pigs they raised. But there was certainly very little money. Oprah never wore a store-bought dress; her grandmother made all her clothes. Oprah had only one doll, and it was homemade, too, from a corncob.

Although her grandmother bought shoes for her, neighbors who didn't go to church probably thought Oprah didn't have any. Partly because she liked to, and partly to save her patent leather shoes for Sunday, Oprah went barefoot the rest of the week. It was a natural thing to do in the country. Oprah's grandmother cared for her very well, and people recall that Oprah and her grandmother always looked clean and neat. Oprah's grandmother was a proud woman.

As Oprah looks back on those years, she remembers the anxiety and uncertainty of being very poor. But that is not her main regret. Homemade dresses and corncob dolls weren't so bad. The worst part of the Mississippi years was being lonely and feeling unloved and unwanted. Even as a very small child, Oprah knew that every child was supposed to have a mother and father—and she didn't.

Oprah's parents never married and never seemed to have much of a commitment to each other. They were very young when they met in 1953. Oprah's father, Vernon Winfrey, was twenty years old and a soldier stationed at Fort Rucker, Alabama, about 250 miles from Kosciusko. He transferred to another town before Oprah was born and then moved to Nashville. He didn't know he had fathered a child until Oprah's mother sent him a note.

Oprah's mother, Vernita Lee, was only eighteen years old, and had been planning to leave Kosciusko. During the 1950s, many blacks left the South to seek work in the industrial cities of the North, such as Detroit, Milwaukee, Chicago, or Cleveland. The only large employer in Kosciusko was a cotton mill, and it eventually closed down. With no good job prospects in Kosciusko, and much better ones in the North, Vernita Lee left for Milwaukee shortly after Oprah was born. The child was left in the care of her grandmother.

Oprah's mother had made a difficult decision based on economic necessity, but Oprah understood only that she had been abandoned. Like other children who have been separated from parents, either through divorce, death, or economic conditions, Oprah felt rejected and unloved. She was in turn angry, guilty, resentful, and rebellious. These negative feelings created problems for Oprah for quite a long time.

Oprah's grandmother, Hattie May, often wound up the recipient of the hostility and anger Oprah had against her missing mother. In her own way, Hattie May tried her best and in many respects did a superb job of raising Vernita Lee's child. Oprah gave her grandmother full credit for developing the talents and qualities that led to her later success. "I am what I am because of my grandmother. My strength. My sense of reasoning. Everything. All that was set by the time I was six."[1]

By the time Oprah was three, Grandmother had taught her to do arithmetic, read, write, and recite Bible verses. But many people have tried to teach three year olds and failed. Oprah was exceptionally gifted. There was never any doubt about that in the minds of the people of the community. People in the Faith United Mississippi Baptist Church remember the day little Oprah, age three, got up before the congregation to recite the story of Jesus rising on Easter morning. She told the story perfectly and never became distracted or confused as small children usually do. And she delivered the story with a power that held them spellbound. She was clearly the pet of the congregation, and they often remarked that she was special and gifted.

When it came time for her to go to kindergarten, Oprah found it utterly boring and childish. Most of the other children couldn't even write their own names, and didn't learn to until they were in first grade. But Oprah could—and much more besides. She wrote the teacher a letter explaining why she didn't feel she belonged in kindergarten. The astonished teacher had to agree, and took Oprah out. When she started first grade a while later, she skipped from first to third.

Along with her natural abilities and the teaching of her grandmother, the solitude of farm life helped develop Oprah's talents. She didn't spend her time playing with other children or watching TV. She spent her spare time reading. Books became Oprah's friends and her retreat from a troubled world. When company came, Oprah's grandmother did not want her to mingle with the adults, feeling children should be seen and not heard. So Oprah sat in a corner with her books.

Hattie May had an old-fashioned concept of what it meant to be well-behaved. She was a strong-willed woman, very, very strict, and believed in corporal punishment.

Attitudes of respect and politeness are important to southerners. And if poor white people were expected to show respect, particularly for their parents and their bosses, it was considered even more essential for blacks. Poor, smart-alek whites didn't get far in the South, and for poor, smart-alek blacks, it could be downright dangerous.

In Oprah's six years in Kosciusko, Mississippi, the little town was racially segregated. In the South, laws required separate schools for blacks and whites, separate sections at restaurants and in buses, and separate drinking fountains and toilets. The whites' facilities were usually better. Most blacks did not vote, because they were "discouraged" from registering by the Ku Klux Klan. Blacks who threatened the white establishment in any way could wind up whipped, hung, or having their houses burned.

Although Kosciusko was segregated, Oprah says she never experienced racial problems there. Kosciusko was named for Tadeusz Kosciuszko, a Polish general who served in the American Revolution. He was a passionate man who hated slavery, and he left money in his will to free slaves. Thomas Jefferson called him "the purest son of liberty." It may be that living in a town named for such a man had a beneficial effect on its inhabitants, black and white. Until Oprah Winfrey became famous, Kosciusko's most famous citizen was James Meredith, who made history in 1962 by being the first black to enroll in the segregated University of Mississippi at Jackson.

More recently, the mayor of Kosciusko remarked that in the past, "We had a base of what we called good-thinking people, both black and white. We existed together. We farmed together. We did business with each other."[2]

But if Kosciusko was a safe haven, it was in strong contrast to the rest of Mississippi and the South. And Oprah's grandmother was well aware of it. It was necessary to "fit in" to the world as she knew it. Not to make any waves. To stay alive. It was essential for children to grow up respectful, obedient, not to make any trouble that would discredit the black community—or antagonize the Klan.

So when Grandmother told Oprah as she whipped her that she was only doing so because she loved Oprah, Hattie May was sincere. She wanted Oprah to grow up fearful and obedient and humble. Blacks who were not could be a danger to themselves and others.

While it is helpful to understand that her grandmother probably had what she thought were good reasons for disciplining Oprah, it is also likely that Oprah's whippings were due to Hattie Mae's own frustrations and hostilities. What they may have been, we can never know, because Oprah's grandmother is dead now. As Oprah says, "Those were the days when people whipped you because they could. You got a whipping just because you got on somebody's nerves."[3]

This is a very sad part of Oprah Winfrey's life. She was always fearful, not knowing when she would be whipped or why. She was terrified of the sheer pain and outraged by the injustice, for she says that she never did anything that was really bad.

Growing up poor and black in a segregated Mississippi, it is not surprising that Oprah often wished she were white. Sometimes she envied white girls just because they had smooth, bouncy, Shirley Temple curls. She hated the seventeen awkward little braids Grandmother put into her hair. Oprah even slept with a clothespin on her nose to try to make it grow differently!

But more often than not, she envied white children, not because of their hair, or because they had more money—but because she believed that white children were never whipped the way she and other black children were.

After all, she had seen on TV how white children lived. "Leave It to Beaver" was one of her favorite programs.

Grandmother was too poor to have a television set, but a few times a year Oprah could watch TV at other people's houses. On "Leave It to Beaver" she saw June Cleaver, a loving, gentle mother, and Ward, a patient, kind father. Not only did the children never get hit, no one even yelled at anyone else. When Beaver did horrible things, such as running away from home, his father talked to him and reasoned with him.

So Oprah believed that all white people lived like that. It was only much later, on her own TV shows, that she discovered that white children were whipped, too, and that cruelty and child abuse extend to all races and all economic classes.

As a smart child, Oprah probably would have responded much better to talking and reasoning. As time went by, the whippings began to have the opposite effect of what her grandmother intended. Oprah became resentful, angry, and defiant.

Oprah was slipping into a troublesome pattern of behavior, rebelling against everybody and everything that confined her. Oprah was getting to be too much for Grandmother to handle.

Meanwhile, Oprah's mother, Vernita Lee, had found steady work in Milwaukee. Six-year-old Oprah would be able to attend school while her mother worked. So Oprah's mother sent for Oprah to come up to Milwaukee to live with her.

Unfortunately, things did not improve in Milwaukee. As a matter of fact, things got much, much worse. And despite the talents and energies she was born with, this gifted child who was considered "special" almost didn't make it out of the Milwaukee ghetto.

Downtown Milwaukee in 1952

Chapter 3

THE MILWAUKEE GHETTO

For Oprah's mother, Milwaukee was quite a change from a small farming community in the South. Vernita Lee worked as a part-time cleaning lady, starting out at about fifty dollars a week. That certainly isn't much, but in the 1950s, it went farther than it does today. She was fairly happy, because her work gave her enough pocket money to buy some fairly nice clothes and other small luxuries she could never have had in Kosciusko.

Vernita Lee also enjoyed personal freedom and a social life that she didn't have in a small town. Most of all, in the North there was no official policy of segregation. There were no "Jim Crow" laws—blacks were free to sit where they chose in buses and restaurants, and they could attend white schools. However, there was still something called "de facto" segregation. That is, in practice most blacks went to black schools and lived in black neighborhoods. They were excluded from white society by subtle means—and sometimes by not-so-subtle means. At that time, restaurants, usually the better ones, could refuse entrance to any customers they chose. Many had a policy of excluding blacks. There were many places where blacks weren't wanted, weren't comfortable, and where they were rudely turned away. (Eventually, the courts would forbid all discrimination in public establishments.)

So Milwaukee was not heaven, but it was better than Mississippi. There were jobs, sometimes very good jobs. Small opportunities were there and an indefinable thing called "hope." Cities also provided the safety of numbers. Although the Ku Klux Klan operated here and there in rural areas in the North, it did not operate in the cities.

Vernita Lee made the most of her small opportunities. One was the chance to look good. Oprah recalls that even though her mother was poor, she always dressed extremely well. Oprah thought she was the best-dressed maid ever. When she was required to wear a uniform, she never put it on till she got to work. She would leave the house wearing a suede skirt and high-heeled shoes, her hair perfectly done. She made sure her children always looked well, too.

But living on fifty dollars a week was difficult. And now there were three of them, for Vernita had a second child, born in Milwaukee. She knew it would be difficult but she was determined to have Oprah with her, too. An apartment was out of the question, so all three lived in one room of a rooming house on Ninth Street in Milwaukee.

If Milwaukee was an improvement for Vernita Lee, it was not so for Oprah. In contrast to the peace, the freedom, and space of country life, she was now crowded into one room with a mother she hardly knew and a sister she didn't know at all. Feeling unwanted and being aware of their poverty, Oprah didn't know why her mother had sent for her. She felt she was just an extra mouth to feed.

Oprah was about as lonely as she had been in Mississippi. But on the farm she could talk to the animals. In Milwaukee, she would have liked a dog, but they certainly didn't have the room, and couldn't afford one. So little Oprah, not knowing any better, captured some cockroaches in a glass jar and kept them as pets. People captured lightning bugs, so why not cockroaches?

Living with Grandmother in Mississippi had been tough. Hattie May was not an affectionate person. The only times Oprah remembers being held and caressed were during thunderstorms when she was frightened. Her grandmother would hold her and tell her, "God don't mess with his children."[1] Because thunderstorms are few and far between, so was affection.

But with her grandmother, Oprah didn't have to watch a stepsister getting all the attention and affection she wanted. On top of being the baby, her sister had a lighter complexion than did Oprah. Living in a white-dominated society, many blacks found lighter-skinned blacks more attractive, darker-skinned blacks less attractive. As the two children grew older, Oprah would be classified as the smart one, her sister as the pretty one.

In need of attention and affection, in Mississippi and Milwaukee, Oprah often reached out to adults for approval. This may well be one reason why she was such a good student; by performing well, she certainly got approval and attention from her teachers. But even though her sister was considered prettier, it was Oprah, the smart one, the good student, the avid reader, the charming speaker, who would become successful.

In Milwaukee Oprah continued to do well in school. But as in Kosciusko, she still didn't get along with the other children. The kids at her school were pretty rough, and Oprah was a gentle child who didn't like to fight. Sensing weakness, her classmates began to call her chicken. On one occasion, six children were planning to gang up on her in the school yard and beat her up. They came after her and cornered her. True to her principles, and in the mold of her church, she began to tell them how people threw stones at Jesus. And in spite of that he had love in his heart for them. And like Jesus, even though they were mean to her, she would try to love them and forgive them, and maybe they could get into heaven too. Her speech worked—the kids went away and left her alone.

Talking got her out of big trouble on that occasion. On many other occasions, it got her into the limelight. Her mother was proud of her speaking ability and often took her to recite at church teas and black social clubs. Where Oprah was once known as "The Preacher" in Kosciusko, she was known as "The Little Speaker" in Milwaukee. On some occasions, she earned money for speaking. She was impressed with that, and decided that was what she wanted to do in life—get paid for speaking. A favorite poem was "Invictus" by William Ernest Henley:

> Out of the night that covers me,
> Black as the Pit from pole to pole,
> I thank whatever gods may be,
> For my unconquerable soul.

She was certainly quite the little celebrity at churches

and clubs. But at home, things were not working out. Vernita Lee was having a hard time making ends meet, and she was discovering how hard it was to be a single parent to two children—particularly when one of those children was a rambunctious, resentful child who had been abandoned. One day, in desperation, she appealed to Oprah's father, Vernon Winfrey.

Vernon Winfrey had moved to Nashville after military service. He was happily married. He and his wife Zelma had wanted to have children, but they found that they could not. Zelma had had a miscarriage and doctors advised her not to try to have children. When they heard that Vernita Lee was having a hard time making ends meet by herself, they offered to take Oprah.

So, in 1962, after only a year with her mother and stepsister in Milwaukee, Oprah went to Nashville to live with her natural father and stepmother. She has complained how she felt bounced around from relative to relative, from town to town. She had the impression nobody really wanted her. Or, rather, sometimes they did, but then they didn't. It wasn't very reassuring.

Life in Nashville was yet another big change for Oprah. Her father was very different from her mother, and so was life in his house. He had ambition and was quite skillful at making the most of his small opportunities. He became a barber and got his own shop. Then he became active in local politics and was elected to office. But he began at rock bottom, working two jobs—one as a pot washer at a hospital for seventy-five cents an hour and another as a janitor at Vanderbilt University.

So Vernon and Zelma were not living in the lap of luxury by any means. But their life was orderly, safe, quiet, and stable. They were quite strict. Nonsense was not tolerated and hard work was expected. Because Oprah had been skipped from first to third grade, she hadn't yet learned multiplication. Her stepmother set out to help her catch up with the other students. All summer long, they worked on her multiplication tables. Zelma also made Oprah read—a book a week—plus write a book report on it. Oprah also had to learn a list of new words every week to improve her vocabulary.

Life with Vernon and Zelma was very regimented; Oprah compared it to military school. But Oprah is grateful for it now and admits she is thankful to them for their efforts. Clearly, her new parents were happy to see they had a bright child with such fine potential.

Oprah was feeling more secure with her father. She became more outgoing and learned how to make friends at school. She went to church regularly at the Faith United Church, and decided to become a missionary. At school she led devotions and collected money for starving children in Costa Rica.

But Vernita Lee missed Oprah. She asked Vernon to let Oprah visit with her for summer vacation. Then, when fall came and Vernon returned to take her back, Vernita refused. Because he never married Vernita Lee, Vernon had no legal rights as a father. He wept when he was told he couldn't have Oprah anymore. Explaining it later, he said, "We had brought her out of that atmosphere, out of a house into a home, so I knew it was not good for her, being in *that* environment again."[2]

If it was a disappointment for Vernon, it was for Oprah, too. "I wanted a Daddy when I was in Milwaukee. I wanted a family like everybody else."[3]

During Oprah's year in Nashville, her mother had a third child, a boy. Eventually the father of this child would live with them, this time in a two-bedroom apartment. But it wasn't quite the kind of happy family life Oprah wanted. The baby boy and the light-skinned stepsister were showered with attention and Oprah was ignored. There was no more encouragement or appreciation for Oprah's studies. She may well have felt like Cinderella, having been taken to a ball for one night and then having to return to her unhappy circumstances the next day.

Like many children who are very unhappy and don't get attention, Oprah began to act up. She had been rebellious since she lived in Kosciusko. Now she was more unhappy and misbehaved even more. Sometimes it was just a matter of small, irritating things, such as playing tricks on people. But sometimes it was more serious, like stealing money from her mother's purse.

She was already a sad, confused, lonely child who had been treated badly in so many ways. Then Oprah experienced one of the worst things that can happen to a child. When she was just nine years old, she was sexually molested. The molester was her own cousin, a nineteen-year-old boy. She had never felt comfortable with him. One night when her mother and stepfather were away and her cousin was babysitting, he raped her. The next day he took Oprah to the zoo, bought her an ice cream cone, and warned her not to tell anyone.

Like most children, Oprah had probably been warned about strangers touching her. But in those days, people didn't discuss these things. At age nine, Oprah didn't understand what had happened to her.

It was all terribly confusing to her. It would have been

uncomfortable to tell anyone (such as a relative or teacher or minister she trusted), but it was worse not to tell anyone. Feeling guilty and fearful were only part of the anguish. Because like other children who have been sexually abused, Oprah began to feel that she was damaged goods, not quite as valuable as children who had not been molested. And she was very angry about the injustice of it all. She knew that she didn't deserve such treatment, but she didn't know what to do about it. She became aggressive, taking out her anger on people and doing things that were not in her best interests. She became more rebellious. She was mad at the world for giving her such a bad deal in life.

Again, books became Oprah's consolation, a way she could retreat from a nasty, disappointing environment. In 1967 she attended Lincoln School in Milwaukee. She caught the attention of a teacher, Gene Abrams, who would notice Oprah reading by herself in the school cafeteria while the other students were fooling around. He could see that she was sensitive and very bright. Abrams feared Oprah would not develop fully in that rough school. So he recommended Oprah for a special scholarship to a private high school.

Among all the bad luck in her life, here was a stroke of good luck for Oprah. It was her good fortune to be a good student at the right time. By 1968, the efforts of civil rights reformers were having their effects, and society at large was becoming conscious of the inequality of opportunities for blacks and minorities. Many people were trying to remedy the injustices of years and years of segregation and exclusions.

Oprah always was ready to do her best. She worked hard in her new school, and socially she reached out to the students who befriended her. Actually, the students reached out to her. For they were white and Oprah was black. And in 1968, Oprah recalls that black was in.

Nicolet High School was all white, and located in Fox Lake, a suburb of Milwaukee on the North Shore. It was twenty miles away from her home and Oprah had to take three buses to get there. The only other blacks on the bus going from Oprah's neighborhood to the North Shore were maids.

Oprah was the only black student in the school and she was popular. She was often invited to the homes of the wealthy white students, whose parents were very nice to her. But the parents had little or no contact with black people, other than their maids, and were self-conscious. They said and did silly things. They would make it a point to play records of black singers when Oprah was there and talk about the only blacks they knew of, such as Sammy Davis, Jr.

Even though everyone was very nice, Oprah was uncomfortable. Most of all, she began to be aware of a different way of life, of comforts she had seen only on television. The luxurious homes she saw were quite a change from her poor neighborhood. She saw everything in a new light and became aware of the poverty around her. It was hard for her to be satisfied with her own neighborhood any more, and it depressed her.

Her classmates were actually living that wholesome "Leave It to Beaver" existence of which she always had dreamed. Oprah felt inadequate and began to lie to her classmates about her mother and father. She would tell them that her father was out of town on business. She says, "I told the biggest lies about them because I wanted to be like everybody else."[4] Of course her new friends had plenty of pocket money. They were always going out for pizzas and inviting her. To keep up with them, Oprah stole money from her mother.

If she felt she wasn't pretty, compared to her lighter-skinned stepsister, going to school where all the girls were white made Oprah feel worse. At thirteen, Oprah was experiencing a teenager's desire to be accepted and to keep up with the crowd. But it was difficult when the others had so much more than she. She felt miserable. She was ashamed of her looks, her poverty, and of not having a father. Eating away at Oprah from underneath was the sexual abuse she had suffered from her cousin.

Like many teenagers, Oprah didn't like anything her mother chose for her. Most of all she hated her glasses. They were a butterfly shape that was popular in the 50s and 60s. They were too old-fashioned for a stylish teen of the late 60s. And they were bifocals. Oprah was sure she looked horrible in them, and maybe she did. She was determined not to wear them. She decided to make up a story about their apartment being burgled. She would break her glasses, then tell her mother she was hit on the head and the awful glasses were smashed when she was struck.

Oprah did it. She called the police and then pretended to have amnesia. (She got that idea from a television program.) She was rushed to the hospital. Her mother arrived and was terribly upset. But then she found out that the only thing destroyed was the pair of glasses Oprah hated so much. The doctors believed Oprah, but Vernita Lee knew it was a lie and took Oprah home.

Oprah lied about another burglary later on for a different, but equally outlandish, reason. Oprah had always wanted a puppy, and was finally able to talk her mother into getting one. Unfortunately, the puppy wasn't housebroken and was creating quite a mess in the apartment. No one was home during the day to train and walk the puppy and Vernita decided to get rid of it. Oprah argued that the puppy was a good watchdog and was protecting their valuables. What better proof, she thought, than to stage a fake burglary again and credit the puppy with warning the neighbors. To make it seem like a real burglary, Oprah messed things up. Then she threw her mother's jewelry out the window. The police were called and when Vernita came home she knew right away it was all Oprah's doing. Vernita was furious. The jewelry was recovered, but her mother was horrified at the prospect of almost having lost her precious jewelry. It wasn't very expensive, but it was all Vernita had. She had worked hard cleaning other people's houses to buy it. Oprah's impossible behavior was becoming dangerous to herself and others.

But people noticed only the outside behavior, the lying and stealing. On the inside there was a very desperate girl. Oprah wanted very much to be loved and accepted, and she wasn't finding those things. The puppy was important because it gave her more affection than she had ever known. Having the right glasses was important because they made Oprah feel accepted and admired by her schoolmates. A good deal of the trouble Oprah got into was because of her great, unfulfilled need for love, affection, and acceptance. Often she was angry at being denied those things.

She tried several times to run away from home. The first time was in Mississippi, and several times later in Milwaukee. The last time she stayed away for a whole week. She had planned to stay at a girlfriend's house. They made arrangements, but their signals got mixed up. When Oprah went to the friend's house, she found that the girl and her family were away on vacation.

Not knowing what to do she wandered the streets of Milwaukee. Then she happened to notice a limousine and recognized Aretha Franklin. Aretha Franklin was one of the biggest singing stars of the 1960s. Impulsively, Oprah ran up to her and began crying, saying that she had been abandoned and had no money to get back to her home in Ohio. Oprah was a good actress—and desperate. Aretha believed Oprah and gave her one hundred dollars to get home. That was quite a bit of money at the time, and Oprah was able to check into a nice hotel for a while. But the money ran out and she had to go home. Afraid of facing her mother, she decided to call her minister, who took her home to her mother.

To teach her a lesson, Vernita Lee tried to put Oprah in a juvenile home. Fortunately for Oprah the home was full at that time. But the threat of incarceration had no effect on Oprah. Her behavior did not improve. Like many girls who are troubled and feel unloved and unwanted, Oprah thought she could find affection and attention from boys by being promiscuous. But it only made her feel that she was being used and she felt worse about herself. Oprah was in a losing cycle and didn't know how to get out.

This was a dangerous period for Oprah—the teen years can be especially difficult for troubled youngsters. With all the problems Oprah had had, she was a disaster waiting to happen. She was unhappy, guilty, angry, extremely vulnerable, and out of control.

Looking back on this period in her life, she says that if she had not come out of this environment she would probably have wound up as a poor, unwed mother and just another statistic on the welfare roles. However much she wanted or deserved the good things in life, she was headed down the wrong road.

But that didn't happen. Vernita Lee felt she was doing all she could to help Oprah and it wasn't working. So once again she turned to Vernon Winfrey for help.

In 1968, Oprah went back to live with her father and stepmother in Nashville. This time, she would stay there until she was almost through college.

Chapter 4

NASHVILLE, SECURITY, AND A NEW START

Sooner or later, everyone's luck changes, a little or a lot, for better or for worse. In 1968, Oprah Winfrey's luck changed more than she realized at the time. Going back to Nashville was good luck, just because it got her *out* of a bad environment. But it was more—much more. In Nashville, everything in her life changed for the better. Nashville signaled a wonderful new start where she would put her unhappy past behind her forever. A new Oprah would get everything she needed to succeed and be happy. Within a very short time, she would begin to show signs of her dazzling future. Her climb to fame and fortune started in high school in Nashville.

Very often good luck comes disguised as hard work. And in the beginning it was very hard indeed. Being Vernon

Winfrey's daughter was very demanding and Oprah did not always like it.

Oprah was thirteen and on her way to becoming a young woman. But Vernon did not like the kind of young woman she was becoming. She had been a sweet, bright little girl at eight; at thirteen she was a glib, disrespectful, provocative teenager, the kind of kid who is often called streetwise. Vernon figured, correctly, that Oprah's environment had made her the way she was. He was determined to protect her—from bad influences, from bad people, and from herself. He could see her need to be liked and accepted; he knew it could work for her or against her.

So to make up for lost time, Vernon tried to help Oprah when she was in her teens. His efforts, although belated, paid off. And they came in the nick of time. Oprah is grateful. "When my father took me, it changed the course of my life. He saved me. . . . I was definitely headed for a career as a juvenile delinquent."[1]

Vernon's strength and discipline channeled Oprah's need for love and attention in a new direction. But it wasn't easy. He was incredibly strict. He started with her appearance. Good girls did not wear revealing clothes and a great deal of makeup. When Vernon noticed too much makeup, he would sit down with Oprah and help her take it off. He forbade short, tight skirts and halter tops. Oprah began wearing conservative blouses and longer, looser skirts.

Then there was her schoolwork. Oprah's grades had been falling. On her first report card at Nashville East High School she got several Cs. In Milwaukee she had come to feel Cs were acceptable. Vernon knew she could do better and told her he expected more of her. If Cs were the best she could do, he would accept it. But he knew she could do better, and so did she.

Vernon told Oprah she had to get all As, and if she didn't, she couldn't live with him. That was a pretty big ultimatum for an insecure girl. But they both knew that she was capable, and it really made Oprah buckle down. Psychologists have come to call this treatment tough love. Vernon Winfrey didn't need a psychologist's explanation. His instincts told him what love had to be about sometimes.

Vernon never hit Oprah. His only reprimand was a certain way of looking at her. Sometimes he lectured her or denied her certain privileges. When he didn't have the time to explain things, it was understood that she would obey him without question. There were never any ifs, ands, or buts. Vernon's rules were law. He told her once, "If I tell you a mosquito can pull a wagon, don't ask me no questions. Just hitch him up."[2] Oprah knew what the rules were. She knew what she could do and what she couldn't.

Oprah certainly wasn't used to this. She had done pretty much as she pleased since she lived with her grandmother in Mississippi, whether anyone liked it or not. Oprah's mother tried hard to make Oprah behave. She didn't want Oprah to make the same mistakes she did. But Vernita Lee didn't know how to change herself, so she didn't set a good example for Oprah. Vernita Lee was confused and so was Oprah.

Vernon, however, was straitlaced and single-minded. He talked to Oprah about life and about boys. He told her that if she didn't respect herself, the boys wouldn't, either. He talked to Oprah about having an interesting life.

Oprah wanted to make exciting things happen. She didn't want to lead a passive or ignorant life. But she wanted to be in charge, to know what would be happening to her.

This is a theme of many of her TV shows today, helping people to understand what is happening to them. This in turn helps people make things happen to change their lives.

Oprah listened to her father and caught on fast. In no time at all, the rewards of her newfound discipline and wisdom came rolling in. Her grades got better, she became popular in school, and she began to win awards and honors. She even got her first break in show business.

Getting all As was not easy. It took a few semesters of hard work and many hours of studying. Eventually when Oprah acquired good study habits, it became easier, and she got good grades in much less time. In addition, her stepmother Zelma still required Oprah to read books from the library— five books every two weeks, plus write book reports on all of them. At first that may have had a bad effect on Oprah's grades, because it didn't leave her as much time for her schoolwork. But in the long run it helped much more, because Oprah gained knowledge, a superior vocabulary, and good grammar. This had an excellent effect on her schoolwork, putting Oprah ahead of the other students who only read what they had to. She has said that her broad knowledge and vocabulary often made people think she was smarter than she was.

Oprah read classics and popular books, white authors and black authors. Reading black authors gave her an added sense of what blacks could do. She read *Jubilee* by Margaret Walker and *I Know Why the Caged Bird Sings* by author and poet Maya Angelou. Years later she would meet and become good friends with Maya Angelou, and she says that this book is still her favorite.

Oprah became active in school groups. She joined the school drama club and gave dramatic readings of *Jubilee*.

How did Oprah do all this? She was getting straight As,

doing book reports for Zelma, and also taking part in extra-curricular activities. For one thing, Vernon limited television to only one hour a day—and that was usually the evening news. That too was beneficial to Oprah's future career. In Milwaukee, Oprah had admired Diana Ross on television. In Nashville, she could watch only newscasters, so they became her role models. They spoke clearly, confidently, and without slang or regional accents. She admired them and was impressed by their power and authority. So, by listening and unconsciously imitating them, she was learning to speak well, to enunciate and to use drama. Very soon this would pay off handsomely, and Oprah would get her first job in radio.

Most of all, she was happy. High school wasn't all schoolwork; it was fun, too—full of rewards and good times. Oprah made the most of the good times, all the more because of her sad past.

Nashville East High School had been an all-white school, and there were some racial tensions there. Oprah was one of the first black students to integrate the school. Blacks were in the minority, so it was quite an achievement when Oprah was elected president of the student council. Her ability to be popular with blacks and whites was a portent of things to come.

Oprah also was elected "Most Popular Girl." To make things perfect, she dated the boy who was elected "Most Popular Boy," Anthony Otey. She was definitely a star in her high school. At seventeen, she was chosen to go to the White House Conference on Youth in Colorado. On the basis of academics and community service, she was a candidate for "Outstanding Teenager of America." Her seventeenth birthday party was held in the school gym and the whole student body was invited.

In her senior year, Oprah went steady with Anthony, who was also an honor student. They did all the things that happy, wholesome, well-adjusted teenagers are supposed to do, just as in "Leave It to Beaver" or "The Partridge Family." They held hands in the park and went out for hamburgers at Burger King and pizzas at Pizza Hut. They went bowling, they saw Ryan O'Neal and Ali McGraw in "Love Story," Godfrey Cambridge in "Cotton Comes to Harlem," and James Earl Jones in "The Great White Hope." They went to a Jackson Five concert and saw the young Michael Jackson. Anthony bought Oprah a forty-inch-long stuffed animal; she bought him a T-shirt that said "Super Bad." They went to the prom together, and her father let her stay out till 3:00 A.M., well past her usual midnight curfew.

Her popularity was not an accident. Like many children

who have been transferred from school to school, Oprah always had to work hard to make new friends. She wanted so much to be liked and accepted—she liked people, and they felt it. Still, people could use her. For this reason, Vernon continued to be extremely protective of Oprah—particularly after she became a beauty queen and a teenage radio announcer, and well into her college days.

Chapter 5
A REBELLIOUS BEAUTY QUEEN, A TEENAGE
RADIO STAR

In high school, Oprah was a good student and a hard worker, but she had stars in her eyes. She wanted to be an actress. In those days, there were few parts for black women (they still are few), but that didn't stop Oprah from wishing.

When she was just twelve years old, visiting her father in Nashville, she earned $500 for reciting a poem at a church. That impressed her. She had always liked performing in front of people, ever since she was three years old in Mississippi. She liked getting paid for it even better. She decided then that's what she wanted to do, and told her father that she planned to be very famous some day.

Oprah loved the limelight. So it didn't take her long to join the drama group at Nashville East. That was her first formal speech training. She particularly enjoyed performing dramatic readings based on the lives of real-life black heroines. Sojourner Truth, the first black woman to speak out against slavery, was one. Harriet Tubman, the abolitionist who ran the Underground Railroad that enabled runaway slaves to escape to safety in the North, was another.

Then in 1970 Oprah went to Los Angeles to speak at a church. She saw all the sights in Hollywood, including the Walk of Stars on Hollywood Boulevard. Like so many other tourists, she put her hands in the handprints of movie stars on the Walk of Stars. When she was back home in Nashville, she told her father that someday her handprints would be there, too. By now, Vernon was used to hearing this sort of thing. Oprah never said she *wanted* to do something; she always said she *was going* to do something.

Oprah was eager for every opportunity for recognition, for every chance to be successful. She always was ready to make the most of all her opportunities. That's how her short career as a beauty queen started.

Oprah entered her first beauty pageant in high school. Miss Fire Prevention of Nashville was a job for a girl who was both pretty and smart, for the winner had to go around explaining about fire prevention to people. In the past, the honor had always gone to white teenagers (often a girl with fiery red hair!). Encouraged by her popularity in school,

52

Oprah entered, and won—the first black ever to win.

Her father didn't like Oprah winning a beauty contest. He wasn't impressed when Oprah became "Most Popular Girl," either. To him, these things were superficial and inconsequential. He told her he would rather see her voted "Most Likely to Succeed." (Oddly enough, the person in her class who was voted most likely to succeed has not achieved the success that Oprah has, a success achieved mostly through her personality and her ability to make people like her.)

Oprah entered and won several other contests. Her experiences in beauty contests helped her in many ways. For one, she developed poise and self-confidence in front of crowds of people. In competitions, you learn "how to get people to see you the way you want to be seen."[1] Contestants are often asked trick questions, some serious, some silly, to find out what the girls are really like. So Oprah learned how to think fast on her feet—qualities that would help her in her eventual career on TV.

But Oprah was never a typical beauty queen. She was an attractive young woman with a particularly nice figure. The rest was personality. She could always win the verbal and talent parts of the contests. Most of all, she enjoyed the game and she enjoyed winning. "I decided to be the best and smartest."[2]

Still in high school, Oprah entered the Miss Black Nashville contest and won. Her father could see that becoming a beauty queen was not harming her. So when the Elks Club was sponsoring a beauty contest and the prize was a full four-year college scholarship to Tennessee State University, Vernon suggested she enter. She won the beauty contest and the scholarship. Once in college, she entered the Miss Black Tennessee contest and won again.

As Miss Black Tennessee, Oprah could compete in the Miss Black America pageant in Los Angeles. At this point, Vernon began to get nervous again. Oprah would be away from home in an environment where people often take advantage of star-struck, ambitious young girls. She had her college scholarship now, why continue? Finally, though, when he learned she would be chaperoned by a responsible person, Dr. Janet Burch, a Nashville psychologist, he agreed.

Miss Black America was a big-time pageant for serious competitors. For the first time, Oprah did not win, and it was apparent to her advisers that she didn't want to win. She sabotaged her own efforts by being too serious and too prim and proper. She wore a plain tank suit in the bathing suit competition. In the talent competition, she played an old woman dressed in a black cape that hid her figure.

The beauty pageant was not a game for Oprah Winfrey.

She sensed that right away. She was in college now and both the women's movement and black activism were very strong, and there were many militants in both. Women and blacks were fighting for better opportunities and respect. Beauty contest winners were not much appreciated by either faction.

Her college, Tennessee State, was an all-black university and the civil rights movement had become very militant. By the early 1970s, after the promises of equality, blacks were unhappy with their lack of real progress as a result of recent efforts. Black pride was a slogan for blacks who had long tried to play down their blackness. Everyone sported a large Afro hairdo, and African studies became a growing field. Students were proud, angry, and assertive. Protests, boycotts, and sit-ins were common, particularly at TSU.

Although Oprah wished to be taken seriously and was interested in black history and literature, she was not a political activist. Confrontation was not a part of her makeup. Oprah was a peacemaker. She joined people together and found the common ground between them. This was not fashionable at the time. And as hard as her life had been, Oprah didn't seem to have felt sorry for herself or to expect the world to compensate for the things that had been denied her.

Oprah believed if she worked very hard, opportunities

would come along. Oprah says that when she was fourteen, she heard Jesse Jackson say that, "Excellence was the best deterrent to racism and sexism; that the greatest contribution you can make to women's rights, to civil rights, is to be the absolute damnedest best at what you do. That's become my philosophy."[3]

College was not fun for Oprah. In fact, she says she hated it. She was a good student, but socially she was "out of sync" with what was going on. In contrast to the popularity she enjoyed in high school, Oprah was resented and condemned by the other students for refusing to join their protests and sit-ins. College is usually a wonderful experience for bright, ambitious young people. But because of the political current, Oprah became an outsider who refused to conform. Instead of trying to conform, she was true to her own instincts and she suffered for it. For someone who has always felt a strong need to be liked and accepted, it must have been difficult.

So Oprah avoided the social scene at college and concentrated on things that interested her, continuing to be active in drama and throwing herself into her work. She played Coretta King in a play about Martin Luther King, Jr., written by a TSU student. At a national drama conference she performed dramatic readings from Ntozake Shange's *For*

Colored Girls Who Have Considered Suicide When the Rainbow Is Enuf. And almost every Sunday she performed a one-woman show at local churches. She gave dramatic readings from *God's Trombone* by James Johnson with a group of singers to back her up.

The major reason Oprah wasn't in tune with angry black militants was that she was enjoying an impressive success as a local radio announcer. She had held a part-time job as a radio announcer since she was a high school junior. She happened to be at the WVOL radio studios to collect money for a charity. Some of the persons she spoke to were impressed by her voice. Out of curiosity, they asked if she wanted to hear her voice through the studio microphones. She was delighted to try. She read some standard news copy and some of the executives came in to hear her. They liked what they heard and offered her a part-time job reading news on weekends on a trial basis.

The radio executive appreciated Oprah's good, clear pronunciation and the particular quality of her voice. Even then it was deep, steady, resonant, and confident. It was authoritative, but still rich and warm. In radio, a feeling of warmth and intimacy are very important. With Oprah, you sensed a real, live, friendly person.

Oprah's father didn't like his sixteen-year-old daughter

being exposed to show business types. He felt that disc jockeys and radio people were wild. There would be too many temptations—most of all, the lure of the success Oprah wanted so badly. Vernon allowed Oprah to work at the station, but he kept a tight rein on her during this time. She had a curfew, and Vernon always had to know where she was, and with whom. All the radio people knew of Vernon's strictness and joked about Oprah's protective father.

On the outside, Oprah was confident and strong when she read. A former colleague, Dana Davidson, remembers her as being aggressive and not at all shy. But often on the inside she was unsure of herself, although not showing it. While radio announcing may seem to be easy, there is much to learn, particularly for a teenager. It took her a while to learn the ropes. She set high standards for herself and was often frustrated until she got better in her new job. When she didn't perform well, it upset her. At one point, she was on the verge of tears during a broadcast. But Oprah wasn't a quitter. She persisted and eventually got better. Soon her bosses gave her a heavier schedule. She read news every day after school and received a salary of $100 a week. That was quite a nice salary for a teenager living in the South. She continued to be a straight-A honor student, to do her book reports for Zelma, and to go out with Anthony.

Oprah's job at WVOL lasted through high school and into her first year at college. The drama experience in high school and college helped develop her abilities in radio. As time went by, she became better and better. Many people heard her, including some influential people. One day one of them called her and asked her to audition for a job on television—as an anchorperson.

Oprah had some doubts about going. The station had to call her several times. Although in her senior year at college, she knew she could not have this demanding new job and go to school, too. But Oprah was goal-oriented, and her goal of graduating from college (the first person in her family) was so close. Yet the TV job was a truly exceptional opportunity. She finally turned to her drama professor, Dr. William Cox, for advice. Dr. Cox was amazed by the offer and told her to take it—quick. He told her that a TV job was the reason why people got degrees in drama in the first place. Oprah auditioned and got the job, at a salary of $15,000 a year. She started out on the important 6:00 P.M. news show.

(Oprah did get her college degree from TSU, but not until 1987, after she had become a national TV and movie star. She quietly finished some course work and was awarded her degree. At her commencement exercise, she was the main speaker.)

Today, most TV announcers have to take TV and radio broadcasting courses in college to get jobs. But in those days, you could get on-the-job training if you had talent. And the TV station management saw some special talents in Oprah.

Just as important as her talent was the fact that the Federal Communications Commission (FCC) had established new guidelines for the hiring of minorities, including blacks and women. The Commission grants TV and radio stations their licenses to operate in accordance with federal guidelines. As a result of the new FCC guidelines, radio and TV stations across the country were looking for talented blacks and women to hire.

In addition, many media people had come to realize that their audiences were not made up totally of white males. Viewers were black, white, Latino, Asian, men, and women who wanted to see people on TV to whom they could relate. Station management found that diversification according to their audience increased their ratings.

At that time, there were no black newscasters in Nashville and not one woman, either black or white. Oprah was the first woman and the first black.

The job was with WTVF-TV, Channel 5, a local CBS affiliate. It was a very important job for a young woman. TV, of course, is very different from radio. There were many new things to learn and it wasn't easy. At the radio station, Oprah had the help of a disc jockey, John Heidelberg, who served as her mentor and coach. At WTVF, she had to figure out many things herself, so she studied tapes of newscasts to correct her faults and to improve her effectiveness.

At that time, there weren't many women on TV news. One of the few, Barbara Walters, was very successful, as well as one of the highest paid people in television. Oprah admired Walters very much and chose her as a role model. When reading news on the air, Oprah thought of Barbara Walters and tried to imitate her every move, every nuance.

Eventually Oprah mastered her new job and became successful. Nevertheless, it wasn't what she really wanted. Journalists and announcers are very objective and aren't supposed to express emotion. Oprah's creative side yearned for something more expressive. Ideally, she still wanted to be an actress.

Oprah began to feel restless. Nashville was nice, but it wasn't the big time. Oprah felt she could be successful in a bigger city, also. She started to send tapes of her newscasts to other TV stations in bigger cities, hoping to get a bigger job.

Oprah was still living at home with her father and step-mother. Her father was as strict as ever. Despite Oprah's successful career, Vernon still insisted that she be home by midnight, and wanted to know the names of all her friends. She had fallen in love with a boy who, unfortunately, did not return her feelings. Their breakup caused Oprah to be very hurt. She was inconsolable over this disappointment in her first grown-up love affair. Her father remarked that when she fell, she always fell very hard.

Oprah needed to grow—up and out. It was a combination of her ambition and a desire to exert her own independence that led her to leave Nashville. Her father's discipline and protection had become stifling. Like a little bird, she wanted to leave the nest and try her own wings.

Vernon's job was over. It was a little late, but he had rescued his little girl and done extremely well after all. Now it was up to her. She was ready to leave the nest and, like a fledgling, Oprah would take quite a number of falls before she learned to fly by herself.

Oprah was a member of the East Nashville Drama Club.

Anthony Otey, Oprah's boyfriend, was voted the "Most Popular Boy," and Oprah "Most Popular Girl" (left). Winning the title Miss Black Tennessee earned Oprah a four-year scholarship to Tennessee State University (above).

During high school and in her first year of college (above left), Oprah worked for WVOL. Dr. William Cox (above right) was Oprah's college drama coach who advised her to take her first job in television. The Administration Building at Tennessee State University (below).

Oprah's first show in Chicago was "A.M. Chicago" (above). She was in competition with Phil Donahue, who is shown here interviewing President Jimmy Carter's wife, Rosalynn, in 1979 (below). It didn't take Oprah long to soar in the ratings.

Oprah played the character of Sofia in the movie version of Alice Walker's novel, *The Color Purple* (right).

Learning that she was nominated for best supporting actress for her role as Sofia came as a pleasant surprise to Oprah (above).

In 1987 Oprah received her degree from Tennessee State University (above left), was awarded the "Golden Apple" trophy from Hollywood's Women's Press Club (above right), and was a presenter at the Academy Awards (below).

Oprah is able to think on her feet when she is doing her show, whether the subject is improvisation (above) or segregation (below).

Oprah headed the cast of the two-part television miniseries "The Women of Brewster Place" (above). In New York Oprah visits James Earl Jones backstage after one of his performances (below).

After losing so much weight, Oprah appeared on her show with 68 pounds of fat in a toy wagon (right).

She also talked about the Stairmaster exercise machine she used (above).

Two women Oprah especially admires are Maya Angelou (left) and Barbara Walters (below).

Taping a show on school violence at a high school in Baltimore, Oprah gestures for the audience to quiet down.

Chapter 6

OPRAH'S FIRST TV TALK SHOW

In TV, as well as in radio and journalism, young people usually have to move around. They get their first jobs in small towns to acquire experience. Then they move to larger towns, then larger and larger, with more responsibilities and bigger salaries.

Oprah was offered a job in Baltimore and she took it. Baltimore was a good step up for Oprah. With a population then of some 787,000, it was significantly larger than Nashville, with around 455,000 people. In addition to being the tenth-largest city in the country, Baltimore has a certain conservative, Eastern sophistication. This offered good experience for a girl from Nashville, where TV had a homier, more down-to-earth broadcasting style.

As always, Oprah felt sure she could learn the job in a

snap and be successful. But this time it didn't happen that way.

In every way, Baltimore was a very difficult time for Oprah—a real low point in her life. She was still young and discovering exactly what were her talents. Although the job paid well, it brought out Oprah's shortcomings. But it was an opportunity and she tried to fit in as well as she could.

Oprah's talents were unique indeed, and when eventually she did find her niche, she was exactly the right person at the right time for the job.

But for the newscaster job in Baltimore, there were many problems. For one thing, Oprah found that at her Nashville job she hadn't learned everything there was to know about TV news broadcasting. There were many things she didn't know and it showed. Oprah was being paid well, and her bosses expected her to do much better. She worked very hard, yet did not get the results she and her bosses wanted. This was the first time Oprah worked hard, did her very best, but did not succeed. Always in the habit of succeeding, she didn't know quite what to do.

For the important new hour-long evening newscast, Oprah was teamed with the popular, established anchor, Jerry Turner. They did not work well together and it was apparent to the listeners.

One problem was that news requires strict objectivity. Newscasters may not get involved with or editorialize on their stories. Oprah's style was more conversational, as if she were sitting in someone's living room telling a story. Oprah was a performer, not a reporter. She never had been trained to go out and get the facts of a story as was essential for a TV news reporter. Most of all, although she was highly literate, she was not a good writer. Even with a wide vocabulary that she understood and used correctly, it did not make her a good writer. Nor did she like to write either—and the job required that she write much of her own material.

Worse still, Oprah never read the news copy, word for word, that others had written. She felt her delivery of the news should be spontaneous, as though she were hearing the news for the very first time, as did her audience. In Nashville, she often deviated from the script. As she was reading it on camera, she would use words and phrases different from those in the script. In Nashville, people liked this. In Baltimore, it didn't work. She often mispronounced people's names, country names, and the like. When one day she mispronounced Canada, her bosses knew they had a problem.

Tempting fate, Oprah kept on doing things her own way, getting into more trouble. However, she knew she was striking a responsive chord in her audience. People tended to like her for her openness and vulnerability, but news was news. Eventually, the worst happened. Oprah was demoted from doing the 6:00 P.M. news for which she had been hired.

Her bosses regretted hiring her, but unfortunately for them, Oprah had a binding six-year contract. They couldn't use her as a serious newscaster. Maybe they could glamorize her for another kind of program. They decided to work on her appearance. In explaining what they wanted to do and why, they said her nose was too broad, eyes too far apart, her chin too wide, and her neck too long and too thick.

The station sent Oprah to New York for a complete make-over. The beautification treatment only made matters worse. She got a terrible (but expensive) permanent and within a few days her hair began to fall out. Every day, more hair fell out until eventually she became bald. She was left with only three little squiggles in the front. She couldn't find a wig to fit her, so until her hair grew out, she wore scarves on TV. During this period, she began to overeat and gain weight. This made matters worse.

So here was a young black woman trying to make a career in an appearance-conscious, highly competitive field dominated by white males. She had just been demoted; now she figured that they wanted to fire her. She had been criticized professionally and personally, told her nose was too broad and her eyes too wide apart. Now she was bald and fat.

Today one looks back at this and laughs. But it wasn't funny at the time. Oprah had hit rock bottom. When she tells her audience that she has experienced almost every trouble and humiliation imaginable, she isn't exaggerating. She calls her bald period a time of self-discovery. "You have to find other reasons for appreciating yourself. It's certainly not your looks."[1] Fortunately, she had some good friends who did appreciate her for what she was. She found out who her friends really were.

As a part of the "improve Oprah" program, her bosses sent her to a speech teacher in New York. Among other things, the teacher told her that her problems were somewhat psychological. She was having problems and they were showing. She had lost her old confidence and enthusiasm and it affected her performance. She was not projecting herself enough because she felt uncomfortable about everything she was doing.

In total, Oprah was trying to be something she was not—and she was trying *hard*. She was being very passive and submissive. The speech teacher had experience in New York with theater and TV professionals. She told Oprah to be more aggressive and to get people to do what she wanted. She was playing the big leagues now. She should stand up for herself. "They're going to chew you up . . . you're too *nice!*"[2]

Oprah listened, but was not able to stop being nice. She said she was raised to be a nice girl, and she always wanted as many people as possible to like her. Eventually, she would learn once again to assert herself. She found out the hard way what was wrong for her and—by a process of elimination—what was right for her.

The station bosses wanted to fire Oprah but they couldn't find a way to break her contract. She was not good reading news the way they wanted it done. And she was worse when she went out to cover catastrophic news stories, such as fires and crashes. Instead of asking pertinent (or impertinent) questions of the victims, she would cry along with them.

Finally, the station decided to try her as a cohost on a little local morning program called "People Are Talking." It was a casual half-hour show on which celebrities and other interesting people were politely interviewed by the cohosts. It came right after the successful national program, ABC's "Good Morning America."

Oprah did not go into the show with her usual optimism and confidence. She had learned that she wasn't perfect and could fail, like anyone else. But after a short while into the very first show, Oprah began to feel very good. It was easy for her to interview people. She knew right away that she was good. "This is *it*," she thought. "This is what I was *born for*. This is like *breathing*!"[3]

It's always nice to find something you enjoy doing and get paid for it, too. But it's really nice when other people are happy with what you're doing. And they were. The show's ratings began to go up right away. From then on, Oprah was unstoppable. She was on the way up. She enjoyed an unbroken string of successes that led her straight to the top of her profession.

Her happiness in her career came at the right time, because her personal life was anything but happy. Young men wanted to date her, but Oprah always managed to fall in love with the wrong men. In Baltimore she had fallen in love again. When the young man broke up with her, she thought it was the end of the world. She thought she couldn't live without him. For a while she contemplated suicide and even wrote a suicide note.

Oprah is not the first person who felt this way over an unhappy love affair. She says that she was never serious about suicide. For one thing, she says, she would have been too curious to see what would happen tomorrow. Optimists don't commit suicide and apparently neither do curious people. Oprah is both.

"People Are Talking" had been a rather bland little interview show. But people were doing new things in TV, radio, and the theater, and Oprah wanted to try also.

Nowadays talk shows and viewer call-ins are common. But in those days, they were revolutionary. Influenced by some radical notions of the 1960s and 1970s, people began to experiment with the media and to involve the audience in the shows. Most shows came from New York. Experts discussed things among themselves and with a TV host. People in the audience listened and applauded. People watching or listening in their homes all over the country simply listened.

But more thoughtful people weren't happy with the passive role of the audience. In the rebellious 1960s, young people were questioning everything; most of all, they were rebelling against authorities. They had new ideas and wanted to be able to express them. They resented anything that seemed authoritarian and nonresponsive.

People in the theater were experimenting with flexible arrangements to bring more involvement into the spectacle. They tried to break the invisible wall that stood between actors and audiences. They made semicircle stages and the actors would perform speeches from the aisles. Eventually the techniques of audience involvement began to carry over into other communication media. Newspapers offered columns to people who wrote to complain about bad products or unfair treatment. They created op-ed pages, where readers were invited to submit articles on subjects they felt strongly about. Readers were encouraged to be more active participants in a two-way flow of communication.

People loved it and responded enthusiastically. The new approaches produced some exciting new television and radio. Phil Donahue was a pioneer of this interactive form. His style of rushing out into the audience and asking people what they thought was very effective. In the past, who had cared what ordinary people had to say? Donahue and other viewer-oriented programs became tremendously popular. People cared as much about what ordinary people had to say as they did about the experts. It was very democratic, very American.

This format seemed to have been made for Oprah Winfrey. For one thing, she gave the impression that she herself was one of those ordinary people and not an authority figure. She had a knack for asking questions that everyone seemed to want to ask, and she made people feel comfortable about speaking their minds. Most important, she had lightning-quick reflexes and a quick mind. She knew the right thing to say at the right time.

Oprah felt she was "on a roll." The ratings were soaring.

She had completely recovered from her previous dejection and self-doubt and was beginning to think of bigger and better things. As when she was in Nashville, she thought that if she had been successful in Baltimore and Nashville, why couldn't she be successful in New York or some other big city?

An assistant producer on Oprah's show, Debra DiMaio, was eager for a bigger opportunity, too. DiMaio was ready for a job as a full producer. She sent tapes of shows she had helped produce to TV stations, including WLS-TV in Chicago. WLS happened to have an opening for a producer on their morning talk show "A.M. Chicago," and hired DiMaio. While looking at her tapes, they saw Oprah Winfrey. WLS had been informed that their show's host, Rob Weller, was leaving for a better job. So now they needed a host as well as a producer. Oprah was the natural choice.

Oprah had some doubts about Chicago. People warned her not to go, not because of the wind and the cold but because Chicago had a racist reputation. Chicago was and is one of the most segregated cities in America. Harold Washington had recently been elected Chicago's first black mayor. During his campaign, there was national reporting on racial problems in the city. Oprah's friends and acquaintances told her a black could never succeed in Chicago.

That wasn't the first time Oprah had heard negative reports. But she had always found that if she did her best, she did all right. So, again, she told her friends, she was going to go for it and do the best she could. She always believed the best of people, even racists.

To many observers, black and white, in Baltimore and Chicago, Oprah's success seemed like a real long shot. The audience for WLS's morning show was mostly white housewives. She would be pitted opposite Phil Donahue, who was enormously popular with white housewives. But the station manager, Dennis Swanson, was neither a fool nor an idealist giving a nice black girl a break. He had studied very carefully Oprah's ratings in Baltimore. Oprah had been beating Donahue steadily in the ratings; her audience was increasing. To television executives numbers don't lie. Swanson figured Oprah could do the same thing in Chicago, too.

Bill Greenwald, president of the International Radio and Television Society, holds the award for "Broadcaster of the Year" that was given to Oprah in 1988.

Chapter 7

CHICAGO AND HOLLYWOOD

Oprah was never one to beat around the bush. She learned early that honesty was the best policy. When she was a beauty contestant, the judges asked the girls what they would do if they had a million dollars. The other girls gave proper and predictable answers. One said she would buy her mother a house; another would give the money to charity. Oprah thought for a moment about what a million dollars would really mean to her, and said what was on her mind— "I'd be a spending *fool!*"[1] Her honesty charmed the judges, and she won the contest. In another contest, Oprah told the judges she wanted to be a journalist like Barbara Walters, because she wanted to have people understand the truth in order to better understand themselves. Her experience in Baltimore trying to be something she was not made her want even more to live her life as truthfully as possible.

When Oprah met with the Chicago TV station executives she told of her concern about the racial situation in Chicago. At one point in the discussions, she said, "Well, you know I'm black."[2] The station manager, probably a little surprised, said he was aware of that. Oprah went on, "Well, you know, I'm interested in whether you big executive types sat around and had any discussions about me being black, you know."[3]

The executives told her they didn't care if she were green, all they wanted to do was win—raise their ratings—and they figured Oprah could do it. And win they did. The station manager was not surprised that the show's ratings went up—only at how fast they went up. Within one month of her hosting "A.M. Chicago" in 1984, the show got its highest ratings in years. WLS-TV gave Oprah very little publicity, but the news of her spread by word of mouth. Chicagoans were very curious about this plump, black woman with the bright personality. "There aren't a lot of black people in the Chicago media . . . it was like you could hear TVs clicking on all over the city."[4]

Oprah was drawing all kinds of viewers. Black people were delighted to see a clever black woman on TV. White people who didn't have the chance to talk with black people in depth were curious to learn more about them. Oprah was a real person and many people could relate to her. A former boss, Joe Ahern, said, "No matter who you talk to—black, white, rich, poor, male, female, fat, thin—they say 'You know, she's just like me.'"[5]

This time, instead of her bosses telling her how to do things, they encouraged her to handle the show the way she wanted. She probably would have anyway. This time Oprah didn't use questions prepared in advance by staff members. She did read prepared background information before the show. But on the air she just started talking and asking the questions that came into her head. It looked easy, but very few people in TV can think that quickly. It is difficult to know when to be funny, when to be serious, when to pursue a subject, and when to move on to something else. It's a special talent. Oprah had the quick wit and the experience in informal public speaking. WLS-TV offered her a four-year contract for $200,000 a year.

Sometimes Oprah interviewed glamorous celebrities such as Tom Selleck and her teenage hero, Beatle Paul McCartney. During that show, Oprah suddenly told him that she had a picture of him on her wall when she was in high school and dreamed of him. Then she asked him, "I wanted to know . . . were you thinking of me too?"[6]

Oprah's spontaneous interview style didn't always work

well, particularly when she interviewed people she particularly admired. That included her two idols, Barbara Walters and Maya Angelou. Oprah was tongue-tied with both. It was an important day in her life to finally meet these two people she had held up as models for living her life: Barbara Walters as a professional model of the competent, articulate, confident journalist; Maya Angelou not only as a writer, but also as a black woman who had come through similar difficulties with a spirit, a character, and a love of life that were made better because of her hardships.

Often the shows covered subjects of social, political, or personal importance. Sometimes people's very personal problems were exposed on TV, and it was often helpful to viewers with similar problems. This has come to be called TV therapy, and has been criticized by mental health professionals. Oprah now tries to avoid playing the part of a therapist, because TV is not the proper setting. But it is in these kinds of shows that Oprah has proven most exceptional. Instead of a glamorous person from a middle or upper-class background saying, "I feel sorry for you," Oprah can say, "Yes, I understand, it happened to me too." Her producer, Debra DiMaio, commented: "Oprah has had such an incredible life that, no matter what topic we do, it's usually something that has happened to her, in some way or another."[7]

Audience response to Oprah's shows was enthusiastic. After a show on child sexual abuse, more than eight hundred people called the station to thank her for discussing it. Many people ask for help. The show receives thousands of letters, and while they can't answer each one individually, they try to suggest some source of help.

After seven months, the show was expanded from a half hour to an hour. Even though Oprah was on the air for only an hour, there were hours of behind-the-scenes work. After each show, she would shake hands with the people in the audience and then prepare for upcoming shows. Four evenings a week, there were speeches before various social and civic groups, with emphasis on young people. Oprah was partly building an audience and partly helping as an important role model for young people, just as Barbara Walters and Maya Angelou had been for her when she was young.

The work schedule didn't leave much time for leisure. Her friends tended to be the people she worked with. Oprah says, "We work and we go out to dinner and talk about work. Then we go home and we're back here about seven-thirty in the morning. This is all I do. I do this and I do it till I drop. I work, and on weekends I go as many places as I can to speak."[8]

Certain movie producers were looking for an overweight

black woman to play an important role in an upcoming movie based on Alice Walker's best-selling novel, *The Color Purple*. One of the movie's producers happened to be in Chicago for only six hours. He happened to turn on the TV, saw Oprah, and in an instant decided she was right for the part of Sophia. The producer was Quincy Jones, a respected composer and record producer. Oprah was contacted to make a screen test. Oprah went to Hollywood, tested, and got the part.

Oprah had read *The Color Purple* some time before. When she was in Baltimore, she would buy all the Sunday papers and read the book reviews first. When she read the first review of *The Color Purple*, she ran out to buy it. She loved it and bought copies for all her friends, too.

The movie was quite successful, a box-office hit. It was startling and thought-provoking. It depicted black women who were abused by black men, as well as by white society. White society was used to these accusations, but black men were not, and many picketed the movie. For black men who have to fight every day against negative stereotypes, they were incensed that black women should contribute to the image of them as brutal. Many complained that there were no good black men in the film. Oprah, among others, defended the movie because it was in fact based on a true story, and it emphasized how people could triumph over bad circumstances.

Oprah was nominated for an Academy Award for best supporting actress. Another actress in "The Color Purple," Margaret Avery, was nominated also. Neither won, but it was very impressive to be nominated.

Oprah had taken a leave of absence from her TV show to make "The Color Purple" and took another one to make "Native Son." It was based on a novel by Richard Wright, set in Chicago in the 1940s. She played a small role as the mother of the hero, a young man who accidentally kills a white woman. This movie was not successful and was never widely distributed.

Oprah decided to start her own production company to make the kind of movies, documentaries, and TV specials she thought should be made. She called it Harpo Productions. Harpo is Oprah spelled backward.

Her talk show was still only a local show in Chicago. But her appearance in "The Color Purple" had given Oprah national exposure and added to her popularity on TV. In 1985, the show's name was changed from "A.M. Chicago" to "The Oprah Winfrey Show." By November 1985, Oprah's audience had grown to twice the size of "The Phil Donahue Show." The show was nationally syndicated in 1986. Oprah traveled around the country to promote her show.

Just six months after it had become nationally known, Oprah took her show to Forsyth County, Georgia, an area that had excluded blacks for seventy years. Blacks were protesting and there had been confrontations. In the broadcast from Forsyth, Oprah talked to people who were openly racist. The show received excellent ratings, in addition to providing a national forum for one of this country's biggest problems—racism.

It was certainly a time of significant progress for blacks on TV. If blacks weren't getting parts in movies, a few were doing quite well on TV. In fact some were doing very well indeed. Bill Cosby had the highest-rated TV show in prime time, and Bryant Gumbel was cohosting the highest-rated TV morning show, NBC's "Today Show."

At this point, Oprah took a nostalgic trip back to Nashville to see her father. They went to Kosciusko together to see old friends and old places. It must have been hard for Oprah to grasp, to see how incredibly far she had come and how many fields she had conquered. She was extremely happy, and wondered if things could get better. They did.

In 1988, she was able to overcome a very personal problem—her weight. The difficulties with her diets had been the subject of many of her shows. Most people agree that her being overweight endeared her to many viewers, whether they had weight problems themselves or not. Used to seeing perfect, slim people on television, an imperfect person was a refreshing change.

But Oprah wasn't happy about it. After going on dozens of diets, she found a program that worked. Her motivation to lose weight was partly professional. There were better roles available for attractive young women and she wanted to play them. In "The Color Purple," "Native Son," and "The Women of Brewster Place," she had played fat, dumpy, old black women. If she were going to continue her acting career, she had to be more versatile. It certainly must have been difficult to see herself on screen as an ugly old woman so often. She was tired of it. As long as she was fat, she would be typecast and would never get different roles. So Oprah lost weight.

And last but not least, Oprah has gotten her private life in order. After many years of stormy love affairs that left her feeling sad and lonely, she seems to have learned how to choose boyfriends who treat her well and make her happy. She has learned how to handle herself as well in her personal life as in her public career.

The undisputed queen of talk shows seems to have it all. And "all" is what she wanted. Certainly having a positive vision of the future has helped her through some tough times.

Chapter 8

BEING SUCCESSFUL

To be a self-made millionaire is quite an achievement for anyone. To become a millionaire before the age of thirty-five is more impressive yet. But for a black woman from an extremely disadvantaged background, it's astonishing. Oprah Winfrey has come a very long way from her beginnings in Mississippi.

She has a right to be proud of her accomplishments. Oprah has achieved success and wealth honestly and honorably, without compromising ideals or principles. She has cheated no one. She has been her own person.

But many people who have achieved so much so early in life have found their success hard to handle. For one thing, it's hard to stay at the top. Oprah seems well aware of the pitfalls she faces, and tries to keep a level head. In the early years, she had confidence that her TV show would do well. But if it didn't, she said, "I will do well . . . because I am not defined by a show."[1] She always felt she would be successful, if not as a talk show host, then at something else. Certainly, ambitious people who communicate well do succeed in any number of careers.

Many people who have become successful and rich were driven by a desire to compensate for the unhappiness and poverty they experienced when they were young. Often, even with wealth and fame, some insecurity remains. To cope with virtually all of her problems, past and present, Oprah counts on the support of her friends. As a teenager in Milwaukee, she was not too careful in her choice of friends. She has learned to be selective. When times were rough, and she couldn't count on the support and encouragement of a family, she has sought out good friends.

During those difficult days in Baltimore when her career wasn't going well, and she became bald, Oprah still had some good friends on whom she could rely. If she was in tears, she could call one of her friends in the middle of the night, if necessary. She has a special friend, Gayle King Bumpus, whom she met at the TV station in Baltimore. Although Gayle now works as a TV anchor in the east, they still talk on long-distance telephone as often as three times a day—sometimes about important things and sometimes just to talk.

Maya Angelou is another close friend and counselor. Oprah turns to Quincy Jones for career advice.

She feels so strongly about friendship she even made a short television documentary on the subject. Friends agree that the emotional scars of early childhood still have left her vulnerable. Nevertheless, Oprah bears no ill will toward people in her past—her grandmother for her abuse, or both parents for abandoning her. She has come to understand the times and the circumstances they lived in and to feel that all did what they knew how to do at the time.

The times Oprah herself lived in were pivotal to her own evolution. If she had been born twenty years sooner, she might not have achieved so much. Forty years sooner, success would have been out of the question. Although not politically active, she acknowledges the importance of political movements that paved the way for her.

The very year Oprah was born, 1954, marked the beginning of better opportunities for blacks. In *Brown v. Board of Education*, the Supreme Court ruled that segregation in public schools was unconstitutional. Court-ordered desegregation of schools began all over the South and spread to other areas as well. In 1957 the United States Congress passed legislation to protect the voting rights of blacks. Soon blacks were being elected to public offices and blacks were becoming a powerful voting block to effect changes.

Oprah was eight when the Reverend Martin Luther King, Jr., made his famous "I Have a Dream" speech in Washington, D.C. Two hundred thousand people gathered in Washington to demonstrate for equality. Oprah was ten when Congress passed legislation to prohibit job discrimination, paving the way for the hiring of blacks, women, and other minorities—including Oprah Winfrey.

Although Oprah was never interested in active politics, she was always interested in black history. As a teenager, she read everything she could find, particularly about the lives of heroic black women in the South. She was acutely aware of the trials and tribulations of those who preceded her.

Rather than feeling sorry for herself for the hardships of her childhood, she says she feels blessed. She considers her talent itself a blessing, and is grateful for having been able to profit from her opportunities. Oprah shares her wealth on a personal level, rewarding her staff generously and lavishing gifts on her family and friends.

She has given generously to many worthy causes. With education high on her list, Oprah has established scholarships at her alma mater, Tennessee State University in Nashville. Not surprisingly, they are named the Vernon Winfrey Scholarships. After all, it was her father who spurred her on to academic excellence and a wonderful future. She contributes $250,000 every year to the fund. She supports other educational efforts, including help to students in the performing arts.

Most important, Oprah gives a great deal of time and energies to help young people. Remembering the hard times, the temptations, and the confusion of her own youth, she wants to be a positive influence in the lives of young people, often speaking to groups of young people in churches, YMCAs, or shelters for runaway teens and battered women.

In 1985 she founded a group called Little Sisters to help eleven-year-old girls who lived at Chicago's Cabrini–Green housing project. Cabrini–Green is a difficult place to grow up in; many people are caught in a welfare cycle, and drugs and gangs are rampant. A lot of people who grew up at Cabrini–Green have gone on to become successful, but the odds were certainly against them.

Oprah joined with other prominent black women so the girls would have some exemplary role models. On their first trip together, the girls assumed that the famous Oprah Winfrey would take them someplace glamorous. She took them to the library and signed them all up for library cards.

Her message was clear: this is a way to help yourself and change your life. Look at me—it helped me.

In one way or another, Oprah is always telling people that they can change their lives for the better. And they should try to. It's hard to find a more convincing example than Oprah Winfrey.

In 1989 Oprah poses with the staff of her new restaurant in Chicago, The Eccentric.

Oprah Winfrey 1954-

1954 Oprah Winfrey is born in Kosciusko, Mississippi, on January 29. U.S. Supreme Court, in *Brown v. Board of Education*, rules that segregation by color in public schools is a violation of the 14th Amendment. Roger Bannister of Great Britain breaks the 4-minute mile, running the mile in 3 minutes, 59.4 seconds.

1955 Blacks in Montgomery, Alabama, boycott segregated bus lines. Commercial TV broadcasting begins in Great Britain. Jonas Salk develops the polio vaccine.

1956 Martin Luther King, Jr., emerges as the leader of the campaign for desegregation. Dwight D. Eisenhower is reelected president of U.S.

1957 The United States Civil Rights Act establishes a commission to investigate denials of civil rights. Troops are used to keep order during attempted school segregation in Little Rock, Arkansas.

1958 Tension grows in U.S. as desegregation of schools is attempted in the South. The Supreme Court orders that black children must be admitted to Little Rock schools. NASA, the National Aeronautic and Space Administration, is established. Alaska becomes the 49th state.

1959 Hawaii becomes the 50th state.

1960 Oprah Winfrey goes to live in Milwaukee with her mother and stepsister. During the next eight years Oprah moves back and forth between Milwaukee and her father's home in Nashville, Tennessee. John F. Kennedy is elected president of the U.S. Mrs. Bandaranaike of Ceylon (now Sri Lanka) becomes the first woman prime minister. *To Kill a Mockingbird* by Harper Lee is published. The American Heart Association associates higher death rate from heart attacks with smoking of cigarettes.

1961 "Freedom Riders," white and black liberals organized to test and force integration in the South, are attacked and beaten by white citizens.

1962 James Meredith, a black applicant, is denied admission to the University of Mississippi. U.S. marshals and 3,000 soldiers suppress riots when Meredith arrives on campus to begin classes. Reverend Martin Luther King, Jr., makes his famous "I have a Dream" speech in Washington, D.C., where 200,000 people gather to march for equality. The London *Sunday Times* issues its first color supplement.

1963 Riots, beatings by whites and police, and maltreatment by officials mark civil rights demonstrations in Birmingham, Alabama, culminating in the arrest of Martin Luther King, Jr. 200,000 Freedom Marchers descend on Washington, D.C., to demonstrate. President Kennedy is assassinated. Lyndon B. Johnson becomes president.

1964 Lyndon B. Johnson is elected to continue as president; he institutes the War on Poverty. The Equal Opportunity Act passes. The 24th Amendment to the U.S. constitution abolishing the poll tax is ratified. Martin Luther King, Jr., wins the Nobel Peace Prize. Nelson Mandela is sentenced to life imprisonment in South Africa.

1965 Violence breaks out in Selma, Alabama, as Reverend Martin Luther King, Jr., leads processions of 4,000 civil rights demonstrators from Selma to Montgomery, Alabama.

1966 Edward Brooke, a Republican from Massachusetts, becomes the first black senator. Color TV becomes popular.

1968 Oprah goes to Nashville to live with her father and stepmother until she leaves school Reverend Martin Luther King, Jr., leader of the civil rights movement, is assassinated in Memphis, Tennessee. Richard M. Nixon is elected president of the U.S.

1969 The Surpeme Court rules that segregation must end in schools.

1970 Alice Walker's first novel, *The Third Life of George Copeland*, is published.

1971 The 26th Amendment to the U.S. constitution lowers the voting age to 18.

1972 Richard Nixon is reelected president of the U.S. in a near-record landslide. District of Columbia police arrest five men inside the Democratic National Headquarters in the Watergate Hotel—beginning the "Watergate Affair."

1973 Nixon's vice-president, Spiro Agnew, resigns in an income tax scandal; he is replaced by Gerald R. Ford. Five out of seven Watergate defendants plead guilty.

1974 The Federal Communications Commission establishes new guidelines to encourage the hiring of blacks and minorities. President Nixon resigns and Gerald Ford becomes president.

1975 Blacks in South Africa battle armed policemen as waves of rioting and violence against South Africa's apartheid policy spread.

1976 Jimmy Carter is elected U.S. president. The U.S. marks the start of its American Revolution Bicentennial with ceremonies at the Old North Church in Boston. Alice Walker writes *Meridian*. Alex Haley writes *Roots*.

1977 *Roots* appears on TV as a mini-series.

1978 The first test-tube baby is born.

1980 Ronald Reagan wins the presidency in a landslide and is the first candidate since Franklin D. Roosevelt to defeat an incumbent.

1981 Sandra Day O'Connor becomes the first woman member of the U.S. Supreme Court. The first official mention of AIDS is made in the U.S. by the Centers for Disease Control in Atlanta.

1982 *The Color Purple* by Alice Walker is published; Walker receives the Pulitzer Prize and the American Book Award.

1983 In a smooth journey of the space shuttle *Challenger*, Sally Ride becomes the first American woman in space.

1984 President Reagan wins reelection.

1985 "A.M. Chicago" becomes "The Oprah Winfrey Show." Oprah plays the role of Sofia in the movie "The Color Purple." Oprah starts a group called Little Sisters to help young girls in a Chicago housing project, Cabrini Green.

1986 "The Oprah Winfrey Show" becomes nationally syndicated.

1987 Oprah and "The Oprah Winfrey Show" win an Emmy Award. Oprah is named outstanding talk/service show host. Oprah receives her degree from Tennessee State University.

1988 Oprah goes on a diet and loses weight. George Bush is elected president of the U.S.

1990 Lawrence Douglas Wilder of Virginia becomes the first black U.S. governor. Nelson Mandela is released from prison after serving over twenty-seven years.

ACKNOWLEDGMENTS

The editors would like to acknowledge use of excerpted material from the following works:

Oprah! by Robert Waldron. Copyright © 1987 by Robert Waldron. Published by St. Martin's Press, Inc., New York, New York. Reprinted by permission.

Quotes from EVERYBODY LOVES OPRAH! *Her Remarkable Life Story* by Norman King. Copyright © 1987 by Bill Adler Books. Published by William Morrow & Co., New York, New York. Reprinted by permission.

NOTES

Chapter 2 BEGINNING IN MISSISSIPPI
1. Norman King, *Everybody Loves OPRAH!: Her Remarkable Life Story* (New York: Quill, William Morrow, 1987): 35
2. Robert Waldron, *Oprah!* (New York, St. Martin's Press, 1987): 15
3. Ibid., 21

Chapter 3 THE MILWAUKEE GHETTO
1. King, *Everybody Loves OPRAH!: Her Remarkable Life Story*, 33
2. Ibid., 43
3. Ibid.
4. Ibid.

Chapter 4 NASHVILLE, SECURITY, AND A NEW START
1. Waldron, *Oprah!*, 43
2. Ibid., 42-43

Chapter 5 A REBELLIOUS BEAUTY QUEEN, A TEENAGE RADIO STAR
1. Waldron, *Oprah!*, 70

2. Ibid., 68
3. King, *Everybody Loves OPRAH!: Her Remarkable Life Story*, 74

Chapter 6 OPRAH'S FIRST TV TALK SHOW
1. King, *Everybody Loves OPRAH!: Her Remarkable Life Story*, 91
2. Ibid., 93
3. Ibid., 96

Chapter 7 CHICAGO AND HOLLYWOOD
1. King, *Everybody Loves OPRAH!: Her Remarkable Life Story*, 64
2. Waldron, *Oprah!*, 109
3. Ibid.
4. Ibid., 114
5. Ibid., 143
6. Ibid., 120
7. Ibid., 121
8. Ibid., 146

Chapter 8 BEING SUCCESSFUL
1. King, *Everybody Loves OPRAH!: Her Remarkable Life Story*, 170

INDEX- *Page numbers in boldface type indicate illustrations.*

About the Author

Margaret Beaton, a native of Chicago, earned her bachelor's degree from Northeastern Illinois University and also did graduate work in French literature at the University of Chicago. She began her career in publishing and advertising.

In 1973, she moved to Paris and worked on the staff of UNESCO, the United Nations Educational, Scientific, and Cultural Organization. For six years, she helped implement programs in education, science, culture, and human rights around the world. The experience of working on an international team, as well as her extensive travel in Europe, Morocco, Egypt, and Kenya, left her with a lively interest in international affairs, and a commitment to furthering goals of international understanding.

After her return to Chicago, Ms. Beaton taught briefly, and since then has worked as a writer and consultant in publishing, direct marketing, and fund-raising.